Ultimate 70s Songs!

Exclusive Distributors:
Music Sales Limited
8/9 Frith Street, London W1D 3JB, England.
Music Sales Pty Limited
120 Rothschild Avenue, Rosebery, NSW 2018, Australia.

Order No. AM971619
ISBN 0-7119-8999-0
This book © Copyright 2002 by Wise Publications

Compiled by Nick Crispin
Music arranged by Derek Jones and Jack Long
Music processed by Paul Ewers Music Design
Cover design by Chloë Alexander
Printed and bound in Malta by Interprint Limited

Your Guarantee of Quality
As publishers, we strive to produce every book to the highest
commercial standards.
This book has been carefully designed to minimise awkward page
turns and to make playing from it a real pleasure.
Particular care has been given to specifying acid-free, neutral-sized
paper made from pulps which have not been elemental chlorine
bleached. This pulp is from farmed sustainable forests and was
produced with special regard for the environment.
Throughout, the printing and binding have been planned to ensure a
sturdy, attractive publication which should give years of enjoyment.
If your copy fails to meet our high standards, please inform us and
we will gladly replace it.

Music Sales' complete catalogue describes thousands of titles and is
available in full colour sections by subject, direct from
Music Sales Limited. Please state your areas of interest and send a
cheque/postal order for £1.50 for postage to: Music Sales Limited,
Newmarket Road, Bury St. Edmunds, Suffolk IP33 3YB.

www.musicsales.com

Wise Publications
London/New York/Paris/Sydney/Copenhagen/Berlin/Madrid/Tokyo

The Air That I Breathe

Words & Music by Albert Hammond & Mike Hazelwood

Mak - ing love with you _____ has left me peace - ful warm and tired, _____ what _____ more could I ask _____ there's noth - ing left to be de - sired. _____

Peace came up - on me and it leaves me weak, _____

3

Angie

Words & Music by Mick Jagger & Keith Richards

1. Oh An - gie, oh An - gie

(Verse 2 see block lyric)

when will those dark clouds dis - ap - pear?

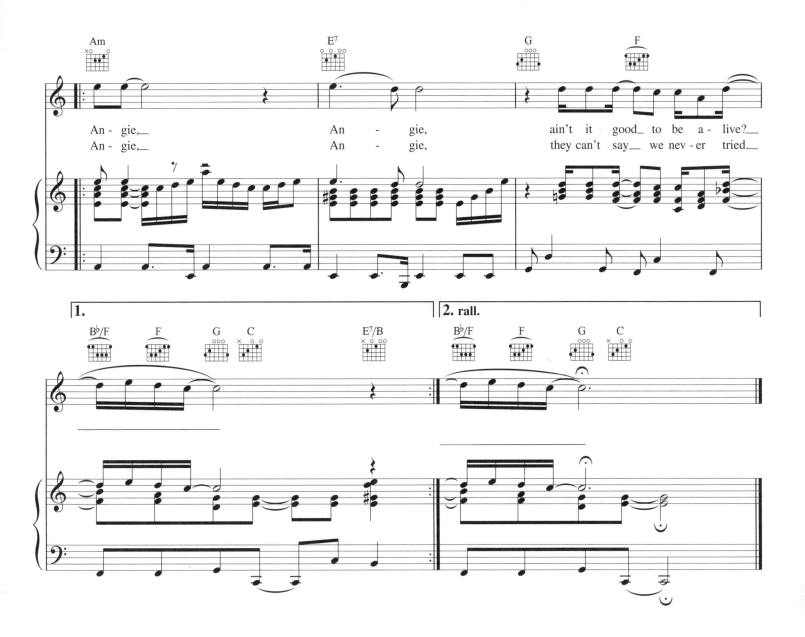

An - gie,___ An - gie, ___ ain't it good___ to be a - live?___
An - gie,___ An - gie, they can't say___ we nev - er tried.___

Verse 2:
Angie you're beautiful
But ain't it time we said goodbye?
Angie I still love you
Remember all those night we cried?
All the dreams we held so close
Seemed to all go up in smoke
Let me whisper in your ear
Angie Angie
Where will it lead us from here?

Verse: 3
Instrumental
Oh Angie don't you weep
Ah your kisses still taste sweet
I hate that sadness in your eyes
But Angie Angie
Ain't it time we said goodbye?

Baby, I Love Your Way

Words & Music by Peter Frampton

Guitar

1. Sha - dows grow_ so long_ be - fore my eyes

and they're

(Verses 2 & 3 see block lyrics)

mov - ing____ a - cross the page.____

Sud - den - ly____ the day____ turns____ in - to night,_____

far a - way from the ci - ty.____

Don't____ he - si - tate_____ 'cause your

love_____ won't_____ wait._____

Ooh, ba-by I love your way._____ Wan-na tell you I love your way.__

Wan-na be with you night and day._____

Guitar

1.

To Coda

12

Well

don't _____ don't he - si - tate _____ 'cause your ___

love _____ won't wait. _____

D.%. al Coda

Coda

Ooh, ba - by I love ___ your way. _____

Wan-na tell you I love your way._____

Wan-na be with you night and day._

Ooh, ba-by I love_ your way._____

Guitar

Verse 2:
Moon appears to shine and light the sky
With the help of some fire-fly
I wonder how they have the power to shine
I can't see them under the pine
But don't hesitate 'cause your love won't wait.

Ooh, baby I love your way   *etc.*

Verse 3:
I can see the sunset in your eyes
Brown and grey and blue besides
Clouds are stalking islands in the sun
I wish I could buy one out of season
But don't hesitate 'cause your love won't wait.

Ooh, baby I love your way   *etc.*

Baker Street

Words & Music by Gerry Rafferty

*fade on **D.C.***

1. Wind - ing your way down___ Ba - - - ker Street,
(Verse 2 see block lyric)

light in your head and___ then___ on your feet, well an - oth -

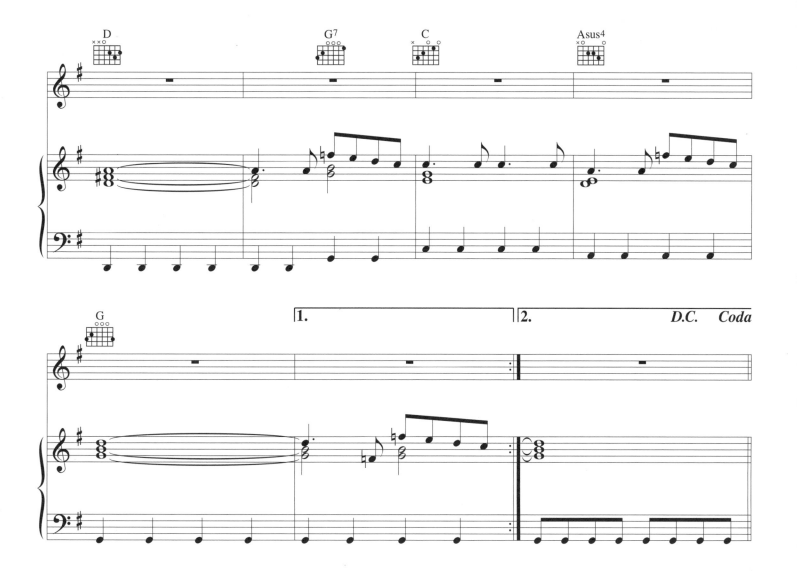

Verse 2:

Way down the street there's a man in his place
He opens the door, he's got that look on his face.
And he asks you where you've been
You tell him who you've seen and you talk about anything.
He's got his dream about buying some land
He's gonna give up the booze and the one-night stands
And then he'll settle down in some quiet little town
And forget about everything.

But you know he'll always keep moving
You know he's never gonna stop moving
His heels rolling,
He's a rolling stone.
And when you wake up it's a new morning
The sun is shining, it's a new morning
And you're going,
You're going home.

Could It Be Magic

Words & Music by Barry Manilow & Adrienne Anderson

Airport

Words & Music by Andy McMaster

1. So ma-ny des-ti-na-tions, fa-ces go-ing to so ma-ny pla-ces where the wea-ther is __ much
(Verse 2 see block lyric)

bet - ter and the food is so __ much __ chea - per. __ Well I help __

__ her with her bag - gage __ for the bag - gage is so hea - vy. I hear the plane is rea - dy by __ the

Verse 2:
The plane is on the move
And traces of a love we had
And places all turning in my mind
How I wish I'd been much stronger
For the wheels are turning fast
For as I hear the winds are blowing
I know that she is leaving on a jet plane
Way down the runway.

And I can't believe *etc.*

(Don't Fear) The Reaper

Words & Music by Donald Roeser

1. All _____ our times _____ have_ come,_
here _____ but now _____ they're_ gone._

La,_____ la, la,____ la,____ la.____

La,_____ la, la,____ la,____ la.____

2. Va - len - tine _____ is _____ done. _____
(Verse 3 see block lyric)

Here _____ but now _____ they're _____ gone. _____

Ro - me - o and Ju - li - et _____ are to - geth - er in e - ter - ni - ty. _____

_____ (Ro - me - o and Ju - li - et.)
For - ty thou - sand men and wo - men ev - 'ry day.
(Like Ro - me - o and Ju -

36

La._____ la,_ la,_____ la,____ la._____

La,_____ la,_ la,_____ la,____ la._____

- by.
(And she had no   fear.)___   And she went___ to him
(Then they start-ed to fly___

Repeat ad lib. to fade

Verse 3:
Love of two is one
Here but now they're gone
Came the last night of sadness
And it was clear she couldn't go on
Then the door was open and the wind appeared
The candles blew and then disappeared
The curtains flew and then he appeared
(Saying don't be afraid.)

Come on baby
(And she had no fear)
And she went to him
(Then they started to fly)
They looked backward and said goodbye
(She had become like they are)
She had taken his hand
(She had become like they are)
Come on baby
(Don't fear the Reaper.)

Don't Stop

Words & Music by Christine McVie

43

Easy

Words & Music by Lionel Richie

Moderate

Know it sounds fun-ny, but I just can't stand the pain;—

girl, I'm leav-ing you—— to-mor-row.——

Seems to me___ girl you know I've done all_____ I can.

You see I begged, stole___ and I bor - rowed,_____ yeah_____

ooh, that's why I'm ea - sy.(*Background*)
ah_____

___ I'm ea-sy like Sun-day morn - ing.
*ah*_____

ev-ery-bod-y wants ___ me to be ___ what they want ___

___ me to be. ___ I'm not hap - py when I try to fake ___

___ it, _____ no, _____ ooh, _____ that's why I'm ea -

ing _____ I wan-na be high, _____ so ____

high, I wan-na be free to know___ the things___ I do___ are right.___

___ I wan-na be free___ just___

me, oh, ___ babe.

D.S. and Fade

That's why I'm ea-

Goodbye Yellow Brick Road

Words & Music by Elton John & Bernie Taupin

Moderately (Swung ♪'s)

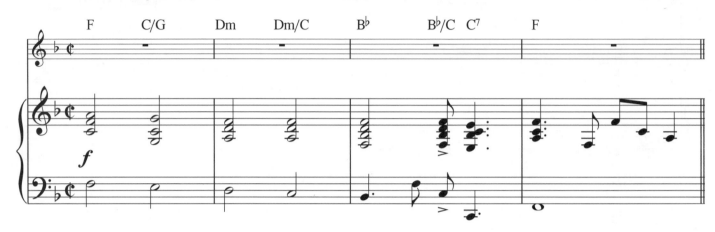

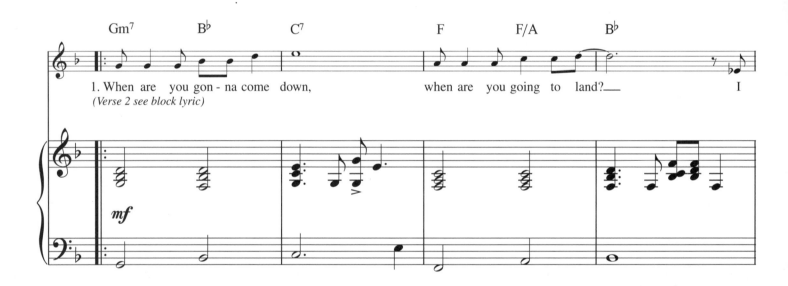

1. When are you gon - na come down, when are you going to land?___ I
(Verse 2 see block lyric)

should have stayed___ on the farm,___ should have list - ened to my___ old man.___ You

know you can't hold me for-ev - er, I did - n't sign up with you. I'm

not a pre - sent for your friends to o - pen, this boy's too young to be sing - ing the

blues. Ah. Ah.

Ah. So good - bye yel - low brick road, where the

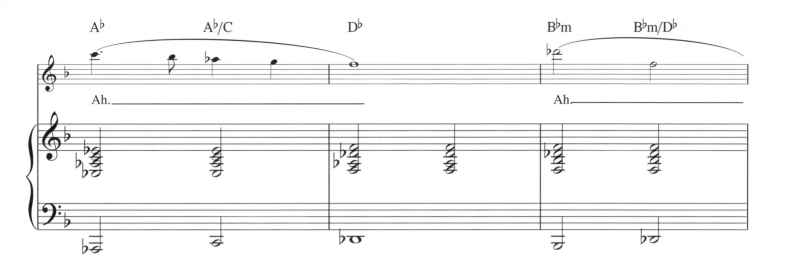

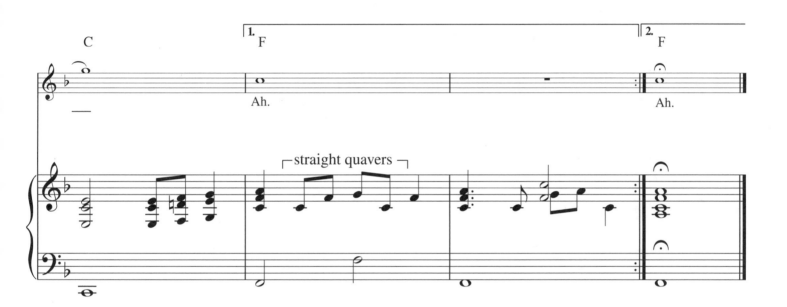

Verse 2:

What do you think you'll do then?
I bet that'll shoot down your plane.
It'll take you a couple of vodka and tonics
To set you on your feet again.
Maybe you'll get a replacement,
There's plenty like me to be found.
Mongrels who ain't got a penny
Singing for titbits like you on the ground.
Ah, ah.

So goodbye yellow brick road, *etc.*

Forever Autumn

Words by Paul Vigrass & Gary Osborne
Music by Jeff Wayne

Like the sun thro' the trees___ you came___ to love___ me,___

like a leaf on a breeze___ you blew___ a-

way.___

Repeat to fade

Verse 2:
I watch the birds fly south across the autumn sky
And one by one they disappear.
I wish that I was flying with them
Now you're not here.

Verse 3:
Through autumn's golden gown we used to kick our way
You always loved this time of year.
Those fallen leaves lie undisturbed now
'Cause you're not here.

Verse 4:
Instrumental

Verse 5:
A gentle rain falls softly on my weary eyes
As if to hide a lonely tear
My life will be forever altered
'Cause you're not here.

How Deep is Your Love

Words & Music by Barry Gibb, Maurice Gibb & Robin Gibb

feel you in my arms a - gain._____ And you come_____ to me_____ on a sum-

sav - iour_____ when I fall._____ And you may_____ not think_____ I_____ care_____

- mer breeze;_____ keep me warm_____ in your love,_____ then you soft -

_____ for you_____ when you know_____ down in - side_____ that I real -

- ly leave._____ And it's me you need_____ to show:_____ (how deep is your love?)

- ly do._____ How deep_____

_____ is your love?_____ How deep_____ is your_____ love?

Imagine
Words & Music by John Lennon

1. I-ma-gine there's no hea-ven,   it's ea-sy if you try.—

No hell— be-low us,—   a-bove us on-ly sky.

you may say___ I'm a dream-er, but I'm not the on - ly one.___

I hope some-day___ you'll join us,___ and the world___ will be as one.__

3. I-ma-gine no___ po-ses - sions, I won-der if you can.___

No need for greed___ or hun - ger, a bro-ther-hood___ of man.___

mf

dim.

mp

It's Too Late

Words by Toni Stern
Music by Carole King

Slowly

1. Stayed in bed all morn - in' just to pass the time._ There's some - thin' wrong here, there can
(Verses 2 & 3 see block lyric)

be no de - ny - in'. One of us__ is chang - in' or may - be we've just__ stopped__ try-

Verse 2:
It used to be so easy living here with you
You were light and breezy and I knew just what to do
Now you look so unhappy and I feel like a fool.

And it's too late baby *etc.*

Verse 3:
There'll be good times again for me and you
But we just can't stay together, don't you feel I too?
Still I'm glad for what we had and how I once loved you.

And it's too late baby *etc.*

The Joker

Words & Music by Steve Miller, Eddie Curtis & Ahmet Ertegun

Some peo-ple call me the space cow-boy. Yeah! __

Some call me the gang-ster of love. __

Some peo-ple call me Mour-ice, __ 'Cause I

speak of the Pom-pa-tus of love.__ Peo-ple talk a-

bout me ba-by; Say I'm do-in' you wrong, do-in' you

wrong.___ But don't you wor-ry

ba - by. 'Cause I'm right here, right here, right here, right here at

Additional Lyrics

2. You're the cutest thing that I ever did see;
I really love your peaches, want to shake your tree.
Lovey dovey, lovey dovey, lovey dovey all the time;
Come on baby I'll show you a real good time.

Knockin' On Heaven's Door

Words & Music by Bob Dylan

I feel like I'm knock-in' on heav-en's door.
I feel like I'm knock-in' on heav-en's door.

Knock, knock, knock-in' on heav-en's door, ___ Knock, knock, knock-in' on heav-en's door, ___

Knock, knock, knock-in' on heav-en's door, ___ Knock, knock, knock-in' on heav-en's door. ___

Repeat and fade

Life On Mars?

Words & Music by David Bowie

beat - ing up the wrong guy. Oh, man, won - der if he'll ev - er know

he's in the best sell - ing show.

Is there life on Mars?

To Coda ⊕

Verse 2:

It's on Amerika's tortured brow that Mickey Mouse has grown up a cow
Now the workers have struck for fame 'cause Lennon's on sale again
See the mice in their million hordes, from Ibiza to the Norfolk Broads
Rule Brittania is out of bounds to my mother, my dog and clowns
But the film is a saddening bore 'cause I wrote it ten times or more
It's about to be writ again as I ask her to focus on.

Sailors fighting in the dance hall *etc.*

Live And Let Die

Words & Music by Paul & Linda McCartney

Slowly

When you were young and your heart was an o - pen book,___

(2nd time, instrumental till ___ *)

You used to say live and let live. (You know you did, you know you did, you know you

did.___) But if this ev - er - chang - ing world in which we live in makes you

give it a cry,___ Say live and let die!___ Live and let

die,___ Live and let die,___ Live and let die.___

What does it mat - ter to ya,

*8va lower ad lib. till **

To Coda

when you got a job to do___ you got-ta do it well,___ You got-ta

give the oth-er fel-low hell!_____

D.C. al Coda

Coda

81

Make Me Smile (Come Up And See Me)

Words & Music by Steve Harley

♩ = 140

N.C.

1. You've done it all,___

F   C   G

___ you've bro - ken ev - 'ry code,___

(Verses 2 & 3 see block lyric)

F   C   G

and pulled the re - bel to the floor.___

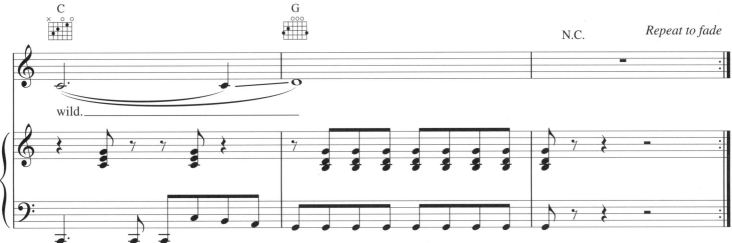

Verse 2:
There's nothing left
All is gone and run away
Maybe you'll tarry for a while
It's just a test
A game for us to play
Win or lose, it's hard to smile.

Resist, resist
It's from yourself you'll have to hide

Come up and see me to make me smile
I'll do what you want, running wild.

Verse 3:
There ain't no more
You've taken everything
From my belief in Mother Earth
Can you ignore my faith in everything?
'Cause I know what faith is
And what it's worth.

Away, away
And don't say maybe you'll try

To come up and see me, to make me smile
I'll do what you want, running wild.

The Man With The Child In His Eyes

Words & Music by Kate Bush

eyes.

Ooh,_____ he's here a - gain,__

the man__ with the child in his eyes.

1.

2.

rit.

Ped._____

Verse 2:
He's very understanding
And he's so aware of all my situations.
When I stay up late he's always waiting
But I feel him hesitate.
Oh I'm so worried about my love.
They say "No, no it won't last forever."
And here I am again, my girl,
Wondering what on earth I'm doing here.
Maybe he doesn't love me
I just took a trip on my love for him.

Ooh he's here again   *etc.*

Mamma Mia

Words & Music by Benny Andersson, Björn Ulvaeus & Stig Anderson

1. I've been cheat-ed by you___ since I don't__ know when,___
2. I've been an-gry and sad___ a - bout things that you do,___

so I made up my mind___ it must come to an end.___
I can't count all the times___ that I've told you we're through.

blue____ since the day____ we part - ed, why, why did____ ____ I ev - er let you go?____ Mam - ma mi - a, now I real - ly know, my, my, I____ could nev - er let you go.____ ev - en if I say____ bye - bye, leave____ me now or nev - er. Mam - ma mi - a,

To Coda ⊕

1.

2.

My Sweet Lord

Words & Music by George Harrison

No Woman, No Cry

Words & Music by Vincent Ford

101

Oliver's Army

Words & Music by Elvis Costello

Moderately

Don't start me talk - ing;
I could talk all night. _____ My mind goes

There was a check - point Char - lie,
he did - n't crack a smile. _____ But it's no

full of __ Ar - abs. We could be in Pal - es - tine, __ o - ver - run __ by a Chi - nese line with the boys from the Mer - sey and the Thames and the Tyne. __ But there's no dan - ger. It's a pro - fes - sion - al __ ca - reer, though it could

Picture This

Words & Music by Deborah Harry, Chris Stein & Jimmy Destri

1. All I want_ is a room with a view:_ a sight worth see - ing, a

I will give you my fin - est hour, ___ oh ___

yeah.   3. All I want ___ is a pho - to in my wal - let;

a small re - mem - brance of some - thing more so - lid.   All I want

is a pic - ture of you. ___

One and one is what I'm tell-ing___ you,___ oh yeah.

Riders On The Storm

Words & Music by Jim Morrison, Robbie Krieger, Ray Manzarek & John Densmore

Ri - ders on the   storm,_____

Ri - ders on the storm,_____ In - to this house we're born, in-

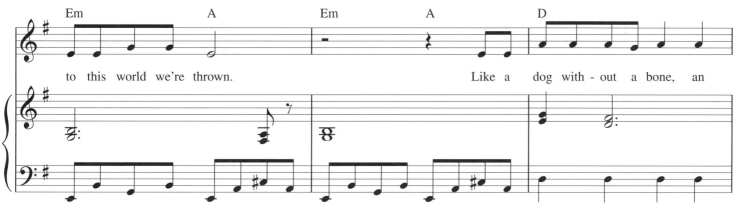

to this world we're thrown. Like a dog with - out a bone, an

To Coda

act - or out on loan. Ri - ders on the storm._____ There's a

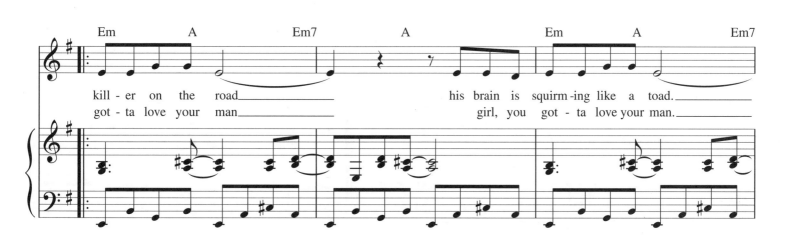

kill - er on the road_____ his brain is squirm -ing like a toad._____
got - ta love your man_____ girl, you got - ta love your man._____

Say You Don't Mind

Words & Music by Denny Laine

1. I re-al-ise__ that I've been, in your eyes,__ some__ kind of fool.
(Verse 2 & 3 see block lyrics)

What I do,__ what I did, stu-pid fish,__ I drank the

You'll let me off this time._____

Verse 2:
I came in to this scene
When my dreams were getting bad
And who rides with the tide
And who's glad with what it had
I've been doing some whining
Now I'm doing some finding
So say you don't mind, you don't mind
You'll let me off this time.

Verse 3:
When it gets you so bad
That a door mat sees better times
That's the time to get back
And think up some better line
I've been doing some growing
But I'm scared of you going
So say you don't mind, you don't mind
You'll let me off this time.

Take It Easy

Words & Music by Jackson Browne & Glenn Frey

1. Well I'm a-

-run - ning down the road try'n to loo - sen my load,_ I got se - ven wo - man on my__
(Verses 2 & 3 see block lyrics)

while you still___ can,___ don't ev - en try___ to un - der - stand.___

Just find a place to make___ your stand___ and take it ea -

1.

- - - sy._____

2.

2. Well I'm a - -sy._____ *Guitar*

D.%. al Coda

3. Well I'm a

Coda

is gon - na save _____ me. _____

Snare

Ooh, _____ ooh, _____ ooh, _____ ooh.

Ooh. _____ Ooh. _____ Oh, __ we got it ea - -

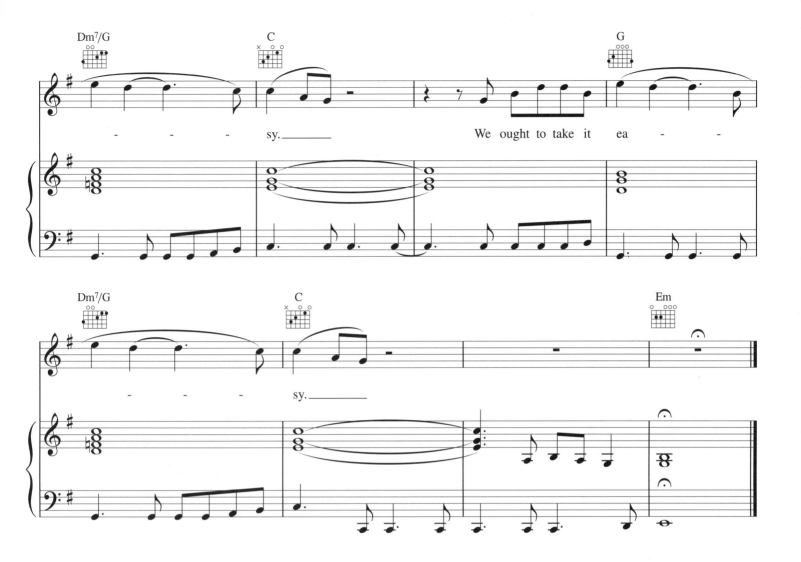

Verse 2:
Well I'm a-standing on a corner
In Winslow Arizona
It's such a fine sight to see
It's a girl, my Lord
In a flat-bed Ford
Slowing down to take a look at me
Come on baby, don't say maybe
I've gotta know if your sweet love is going to save me
We may lose and we may win
Though we will never be here again
So open up, I'm climbing in
So take it easy.

Verse 3:
Well I'm a-running down the road
Trying to loosen my load
Got a world of trouble on my mind
Looking for a lover who won't blow my cover
She's so hard to find
Take it easy, take it easy
Don't let the sound of your own wheels make you crazy
Come on baby, don't say maybe
I've got to know if your sweet love is gonna save me.

This Town Ain't Big Enough For Both Of Us

Words & Music by Ronald Mael

1. Zoo time is she and you time; the mam - mals are your fav - 'rite type, you find you want her to - night. Heart - beat, in - creas - ing

heart - beat; you hear the thun - der of stam - ped - ing rhi - nos, e - le - phants and tack - y ti - gers.

This town ain't big e - nough for the both of us, and it ain't me who's gon - na

leave.

2. Fly - ing, do - mes - tic fly - ing; and when the stew - ard - ess is near do not
(Verses 3 & 4 see block lyric)

show a - ny fear. Heart - beat, in - creas - ing heart - beat; you are a

kha - ki col - oured bom - ba - dier, it's Hi - ro - shi - ma that you're near - ing. This town ain't big e - nough for

both of us, and it ain't me who's gon - na leave.

To Coda

1.

Verse 3:
Daily, except for Sunday
You dawdle in to the cafe where you meet her each day
Heartbeat, increasing heartbeat
As twenty cannibals have hold of you, they need their protein just like you do
This town ain't big enough for the both of us
And it ain't me who's gonna leave.

Verse 4:
Shower, another shower
You got to look your best for her, and be clean everywhere
Heartbeat, increasing heartbeat
The rain is pouring on the foreign town, the bullets cannot cut you down
This town ain't big enough for the both of us
And it ain't me who's gonna leave.

Up The Junction

Words & Music by Chris Difford & Glenn Tilbrook

I worked all through the win-ter, The wea-ther brass and bit-ter. I put a-way a ten-ner Each week to make her bet-ter And when the time was rea-dy We had to sell the tel-ly, Make eve-nings by the fi-re And lit-tle kicks in-side her. This morn-ing at four-

-fif-ty I took her rath-er nif-ty Down to an in-cu-ba-tor. 'Bout thir-ty mi-nutes la-ter She gave birth to a daugh-ter, With-in a year a walk-er. She looked just like her moth-er If there could be an-oth-er. —

And now she's two years old-er, Her moth-er's with a sol-dier. She left me when my
A-lone here in the kit-chen, I feel there's some-thing miss-ing. I'd beg for some for-

drink-ing   Be-came a prop-er sting-ing.   The Dev-il came and took me   From bar to street to
-give-ness   But beg-ging's not my bus-'ness   And she must write a let-ter   Al-though I al-ways

book-ie.   No more nights by the tel-ly,   No more nights nap-pies smell-ing.
tell her   And so it's my as-sump-tion   I'm real-ly up the junc-tion.

1
2

F   Bb

1, 2, 3   4

F   Bb   Bb   F

What's Going On

Words & Music by Marvin Gaye, Al Cleveland & Renaldo Benson

Broth - er, broth - er, broth - er,___ there's far too ma - ny

of you dy - ing. You___ know___ we've

got to find___ a way to bring some

1.
lov - in' here to - day,___ yeah._____

2, 3.
oh._____

Verse 2:
Father, father
We don't need to escalate
You see, war is not the answer
For only love can conquer hate
You know we've got to find a way
To bring some lovin' here today.

Picket lines etc.

Verse 3:
Mother, mother
Everybody thinks we're wrong
Oh, but who are they to judge us
Simply 'cause our hair is long
Oh you know we've got to find a way
To bring some understanding here today, oh.

Picket lines etc.

You're My Best Friend

Words & Music by John Deacon

shine,_ and I want_ you to know_ that my feel-

-ings are true.__ I real-ly love_____ you.__

Oh,____ you're my best__ friend._____

Ooh,___ you make me live.__ Oh,_ I've been wan-der-ing round, But I

still come back to you.____ And in rain or__ shine_ you've

stood by me girl.__ I'm hap - py at home.__ You're my best_

1.

friend._____

2.

friend.

N.C.

Oh.__

Verse 2:
Ooh, you make me live
Whenever this world is cruel to me
I got you to help me forgive
Ooh, you make me live now, honey
Ooh, you make me live.

Oh you're the first one
When things turn out bad
You know I'll never be lonely
You're my only one
And I love the things
I really love the things that you do
You're my best friend.

Ooh you make me live...
(Instrumental)

I'm happy at home
You're my best friend.

You're So Vain

Words & Music by Carly Simon

Verse 2:
You had me several years ago, when I was still quite naïve.
Well, you said that we made such a pretty pair, and that you would never leave.
But you gave away the things you loved, and one of them was me.
I had some dreams, they were clouds in my coffee, clouds in my coffee, and...

You're so vain *etc.*

Verse 3:
Well, I hear you went up to Saratoga, and your horse naturally won;
Then you flew your Lear jet up to Nova Scotia, to see the total eclipse of the sun.
Well, you're where you should be all the time and when you're not you're with
Some underworld's spy or the wife of a close friend, wife of a close friend, and...

You're so vain *etc.*

Moondance

Words & Music by Van Morrison

1. Well it's a mar-vel-lous night___ for a moon - dance, with the
(Verse 2 see block lyric; Verses 3-7 ad lib. instrumental)

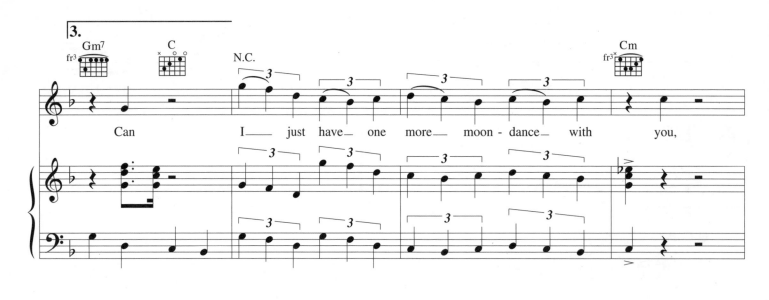

Can I just have one more moon-dance with you,

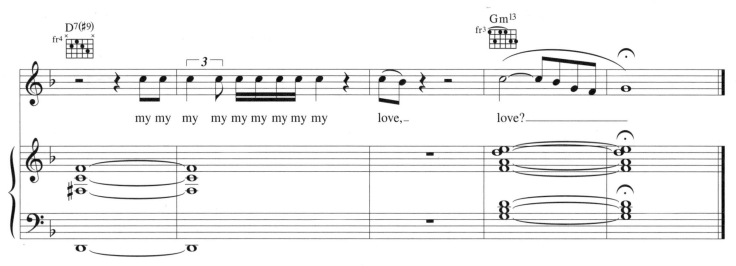

my my my my my my my my my love, love?

Verse 2:

Well I wanna make love to you tonight,
I can't wait till the morning has come.
And I know now the timing is just right,
And straight into my arms you will run.
And when you come my heart will be waiting
To make sure that you're never alone.
There and then all my dreams will come true dear;
There and then I will make you my own.
Every time I touch you, you just tremble inside.
And I know how much I want you baby,
That you can't hide.
Can I just have one more moondance with you, my love?
Can I just make some more romance with you, my love?